INSPIRED

A Narrative and Poetry Collection

Andrea M. Renfroe

Inspired: A Narrative and Poetry Collection
Copyright © 2018 by Andrea M. Renfroe

Printed in the United States of America
ISBN-10: 0-9834520-1-6
ISBN-13: 978-0-9834520-1-0

Library of Congress Control Number: 2016930082

Edited by Christine Lombard
www.cloveeducationsolutions.com
christineannlombard@gmail.com

Published by The Prophetic Pen

THE PROPHETIC PEN
est. MMXIV

"Communicating the heart and mind of God"

Dedication

This book is dedicated to my mother, Katherine Everson. From the beginning, you ensured I was established on a firm foundation in Jesus Christ. When it was time to release me into the world, you did so even with tears in your eyes. But to God be the glory. Your releasing paved the way for a life-altering work only God Himself could do. Surely He has used you mightily in the process. You have imparted immeasurable wisdom into my life concerning the things of God as well as life and its accompanying issues (even if it was what not to do). You prayed for me, you watched for me, you loved me, you cried for me, you rebuked me, you encouraged me, you pushed me, you challenged me, and you helped me to understand my God-given purpose. I praise and thank God for the gift He gave to me in the form of you. You are my Elijah and I am your Elisha. I love you, Mommy!

"As I live, I listen and observe. As I listen and observe, I'm inspired. When I'm inspired, I write."
—*Andrea M. Renfroe*

Table of Contents

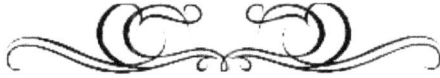

Acknowledgements

Jesus Christ

You are the lover of my soul, my portion, and my rock forever. You inspire me above all.

My husband, Telly

Thank you for inspiring me over the years. Your level head and simplistic yet wise approach to many things in life have helped me tremendously. What you mean to me, who you are to me, and what you do for me (intangible and tangible) serve as a continual reminder that God gives us who we need. I love you, Mr. Renfroe.

My father, Mart Everson Jr. a-k-a *"Everywhere Everson"*

You said a man should get up, if he is physically able, and work to take care of his family. You practiced what you preached. I vividly remember seeing you work sun up to sun down to take care of us. In the midst of working hard, you also found time to enjoy life. Sports, cards, dominos, cookouts, get togethers, watching TV, going to the park, supporting me during my basketball games and track meets, and so much more.

It was natural for you to be everywhere and to just keep going and going and going like the Energizer bunny. Oftentimes I wondered how you did what you did. I guess the Lord granted you "Go" grace.

I pray you realize just how influential your example was for me. You definitely set a high standard. Without it, I would not have a great work ethic and I would not have known to desire such a quality in a husband. I am still working on emulating your play hard example. But I declare I will get there. Thank you, Daddy. I love you.

Taylor and Kijon

Before I birthed A'Mia and Telly Jr., you inspired the mother in me. While you are not my biological children, ya'll are still my "chullen" (smile). It is my earnest prayer that you connect with your identity in Christ, tap into your purpose, and flourish in all you are called to do.

Apostle Phyllis L. Terry

I sat next to her at her kitchen table while she looked over the original manuscript. This published author several times over and powerful woman of God was actually reading my material. I was in shock. In the midst of reading, she turned to me and said, "Honey, these are more than poems, they're stories. You should write introductions to your poems so readers will understand where they came from." Up until that moment, I'd never considered such a thing because I believed the poems contained enough substance to tell the full story and to satisfy readers. However, as I thought more and more about what inspired each poem, it was clear that including introductions was necessary.

In 2009, I started assembling the original manuscript for my first book, *Come Forth*. The process I underwent to birth that book along with Apostle Phyllis' (Dr. Phyl) input challenged me to look closer at the manuscript which evolved into various manuscripts—*Inspired* being one of them. During the development of *Inspired*, I was taken back to the actual points of inspiration: the thoughts, experiences, scenes, and emotions. Not only did the additional writing enhance the life and story of each poem, the journey also proved to be therapeutic for me.

Apostle Phyllis, thank you for taking the time to help me through this process. Thank you for putting your foot in my back and pushing me. The investment and impartation you've made into my life goes beyond what money can buy and what words can express. You have truly been a blessing. *Arigatou gozaimasu!*

All who inspired the poems in this book

Thank you for allowing me to share my perspective of inspiration pertaining to you. The narratives and poems may not have captured beautiful or pleasant situations. Yet, I am convinced someone will find hope, comfort, and inspiration in them. I am grateful for your contribution to my life and to the lives of all who will read this book.

Inspire: "to influence, move, or guide . . ."

Introduction

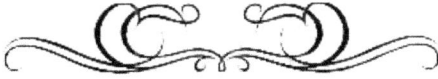

A standing misconception among many is the belief that positive events or happenings are the only source of inspiration. To the contrary, anything and everything can "influence, move, or guide" in one way or another. A beautiful sunset can inspire a romantic embrace between husband and wife, while the same sunset arouses anger in a woman who recalls the evening her husband of fifteen years drove away into the sunset with another woman. Loss of a job causes one to lose hope while it motivates another to launch out and pursue a lifelong dream of starting a business. The death of a child moves one to despair while in another it ignites a passion to save children.

Both good and bad experiences alike have inspired me to write. Most times, the experiences generated a gamut of emotions I was unable to deal with or articulate verbally. However, writing provided a safe and productive means to process my thoughts and helped me to clearly communicate what was happening to me and to others. For years poetry was the primary result of my inspiration.

Although several of the poems herein touch on negative circumstances, they are not meant to belittle, demean, or discourage anyone. Rather, they serve as a reminder that we are real people, navigating real issues, in a real world. Yet, we have a real Savior and Advocate who is ever present to help us and inspire us through it all.

I pray this book gives you hope, changes your mind, and compels you to action. But most importantly, I pray you are *inspired* to live abundantly, love unconditionally, and know Christ intimately.

—Andrea M. Renfroe

I nfluence

N aturally

S preads from

P erson to person

I ncreasing

R espect

E ndurance and

D etermination to pass it on

—Christine Lombard

"Children are the hands by which we take hold of Heaven."
—Henry Ward Beecher

Holding Heaven

I knelt down beside my bed, hands clenched and head bowed. I tried to be strong and astutely carry this life-shattering burden to the Lord in prayer. However, my attempt was disappointing to say the least. All self-strength subsided, leaving me in a vulnerable bear-all position. The dam of pent-up tears broke loose, and wails forced their way through my lips. The pain was consuming and the anguish suffocating. I pleaded with the Lord and begged for help, relief, and some kind of pardon from such suffering. At that moment, my only heart's desire was to experience true comfort and genuine love void of fronts, masks, facades, and lies. The Lord granted my request.

Some experiences are minor and not worth remembering. However, others are seared into our very consciousness because of their significance. The memory of an instantly answered prayer in the time of great need is one I will hold fast to for a lifetime.

My Angels

Inspired by my children, A'Mia and Telly Jr.

I was in need of comfort. I was hurting bad.
My agony was much too heavy to carry.
As tears streamed down my face, I pleaded aloud:
"God, please wrap your loving arms around me."

When I finished praying and opened my eyes,
I saw something so touching and hard to contain.
My children were standing quietly across the room.
They were concerned about their mommy's pain.

They came over and embraced me with their little arms.
Silently conveying, "Mommy, we love you. It'll be okay."
Certainly God heard the cry of my heart.
He used my angels to comfort me in a practical yet divine way.

**"We can teach from experience,
but we cannot teach experience."**
—Sasha Azevedo

On the Other Side of Experience

If she didn't do anything else, Katherine made sure the house was spotless. Certainly, no one was going to be living *"nasty"* on her watch. I remember how she would sit in the vicinity of the area we were cleaning. With a cigarette in one hand and her belt in her lap, she barked out instructions like a drill instructor. She was versatile and very skillful. She could give direction and wield the belt while simultaneously exhaling cigarette smoke. She never missed a beat, and neither did we after being popped with the belt when something wasn't done correctly.

We were dishwashers, baseboard scrubbers, wall washers, toilet cleaners, bed makers, drawer straighteners, floor moppers, and rug picker uppers. That's a human vacuum cleaner for those who aren't familiar with picking up big and small trash particles from rugs with your hands because you couldn't afford a vacuum or you broke it sucking up shoe strings or rug tassels. We were trained to clean house like grown folks. While other kids were outside playing, we were inside cleaning what seemed to be clean already (in our eyes anyway). Nonetheless, we did what we were told.

Back then; I didn't fully understand Katherine's ways. Now that I am a mother, I can truly say I know where she was coming from. While it was hard experiencing Katherine's training, I am thankful for it. Although I am no longer under her watchful eye as I was during childhood, she is forever with me along my parenting journey. It may be my voice I speak with, but it's her voice I hear when I tell my kids to vacuum the rug, take out the trash, clean their rooms, or wash the dishes. While I may be watching over my children to ensure they clean correctly, it is Katherine I see. She chuckles when I tell her of such occurrences and is eager to let me know I've officially arrived on the other side of experience.

The Old Kat

Inspired by my mother, Katherine Everson

When you wash that wall, start at the baseboard and then go up.
Get on your hands and knees to mop that floor.

Them dishes better be washed and put away.
I'm not gonna repeat myself no more.

Put some elbow grease into it so that dirt will come off.
Scrub harder; I can still see some grit.

Don't miss them corners. Wash that rag out.
Andrea, Marquita, girl, gal. Ya'll know what I meant.

Pick that big trash up off my rug.
Shoot, that's how ya'll behinds broke the last three vacuums.

You best figure out how ya'll gonna get it done,
'cause all ya'll got is your hands and that broom.

Them dresser drawers better be cleaned out and closets spotless.
Bet' not nothing be under them beds.

Go get the belt cause I'm tired of talking.
Ya'll acting like ya'll ain't heard a word I done said.

Every time I turn around, I have to keep repeating myself.
I'll be glad when every one of ya'll behinds gets gone.

I hope ya'll have some kids just like you, so they can lay up,
half clean up, eat and drink you outta house and home.

Get outta my face before I hurt somebody.
Bring me my cigarettes, and somebody find my teeth.

Ya'll ain't got but a few minutes. I'm inspecting when ya done.
Until then I'm 'bout to go get me some sleep.

". . . how that not many wise men after the flesh, not many mighty, not many noble, are called: But God hath chosen the foolish things of the world to confound the wise; and God hath chosen the weak things of the world to confound the things which are mighty; And base things of the world, and things which are despised, hath God chosen, yea, and things which are not, to bring to nought things that are: That no flesh should glory in his presence."

I Corinthians 1:26–29 (KJV)

Confound the Wise

It's funny how God uses those that society would much rather forget than to count worthy of bringing Him glory. God employs those who don't have eloquent speech. He uses the poor and castaways. He engages adulterers, prostitutes, liars and thieves— all of whom would appear far from the image of those a great, sovereign, and wise God would dare to associate with.

If anyone were labeled by society as being from the wrong side of the tracks, Katherine Everson fits the bill. Society and the church have written her off numerous times—some of the write-offs being self-inflicted and some not. She is one whom church folk arrogantly look down upon, saying, "What manner of woman this is that toucheth him: for she is a sinner" (Luke 7:39b).

Even though she did not fit the description of what many perceived His messenger should look like, God allowed Katherine to see into the spirit realm and serve as His mouthpiece. God favored her with backside of the mountain, one-on-one training. He unveiled His mysteries to her without seminary attendance. He gave her a heart for the hurting and lost in the midst of major family dysfunction and allowed her to birth a ministry despite facing death twice. On December 4, 2005, Katherine Everson, though perceived as nobody in the eyes of people, was presented to the public as an evangelist, a gift to the body of Christ. In that instant, 1 Corinthians 1:26–29 was publically made manifest. Although people made their declaration concerning Katherine, God had and will always have the last word.

Your Nobody Is God's Somebody

Inspired by my mother, Katherine Everson

With a passionate love for Christ at such a young age,
This nobody was definitely strange from the start.

Righteously indignant if someone spoke ill of her Savior.
He was overseer of her life and reigning King of her heart.

Rivers of living waters bubbled up from her belly.
Diverse tongues poured out from this nobody's lips.

The Spirit of the living God rested heavy on her life.
She was heavily endowed with spiritual gifts.

Shunned for being different; feared for operating in the Spirit.
She was an outcast for not conforming to a traditional church role.

Despite man's opinion of this good-for-nothing nobody,
God was pleased because she was someone He could mold.

Mold her He did through the school of hard knocks.
Holy Spirit served as her chief instructor.

He tested the motives and intents of her heart.
Attacks of the enemy and life circumstances conditioned her.

When this nobody realized what she was being equipped to do,
She stepped forward to share the news.

Had she been fully aware of the coming trials and tribulations,
    She may have opted to walk in someone else's shoes.

For years she suffered trying her best to get others to realize what
    God had called her to be.

Some ridiculed and laughed. Others disregarded the very thought.
    It was something they refused to see.

    How could God call this nobody, of all people?
She wasn't cut from the right cloth and she had a blemished past.

No upstanding husband, perfect kids, or a big bank account.
    To the world, she was merely trash.

She didn't look the part, act the part, or sound the part at all;
    Surely she couldn't be God's vessel of choice.

But God said differently. He deemed her a perfect candidate to
open up blind eyes to His love and deaf ears to His voice.

She still has mountains to climb and tribulations to endure,
    Yet, there is an audience she is ordained to reach.

By His power she will bind up broken hearts and proclaim liberty.
He's ordained her to open prison doors so the bound can be free.

    Your nobody has always been God's somebody.
It's human ignorance--man's wisdom that says otherwise.

God's ways, thoughts, and timing are always perfect.
Truth is what's spoken from His mouth and seen through His eyes.

**"He didn't tell me how to live; he lived,
and let me watch him do it."**
—Clarence Budington Kelland

I Watched Him Live

It was a night I will never forget. Daddy was on another "mission", the term we used to describe his drug escapades. No one had seen or heard from him since he'd been paid on Thursday. It was his regular routine by this time, so I don't understand why we were angry about it. We knew he was going to do it. In an attempt to cope with her anger, mommy threw back a few bottles of Milwaukee's Best and allowed herself to be overtaken by the thoughts running rampant in her head.

Mommy was past tipsy when she told me to get her car keys. She told me I was going with her to find my father. "Huh?" was my initial thought. But my lips stayed glued. Although my body was obedient, the thoughts in my mind were not in compliance. I was thinking, "Mommy must be crazy! She is under the influence and about to get behind the wheel of a car to search for my father, who obviously did not want to be found." I strapped myself in and tried to mentally prepare for what was to come. As we made our way down the road (by the grace of God), mommy looked over and asked if I was scared. I can't remember my response, but I must have looked terrified if she was asking. In a failed attempt to calm my nerves, or maybe her own nerves, she said, "Don't worry; the Lord is driving the car." Surely that was of no comfort for a teenager who loved the Lord, but wasn't strong enough in my faith to believe we were actually going to be okay.

My thoughts drifted to horrendous images of what daddy would look like if and when we found him. Would he be so high that he wouldn't even be able to recognize us? Maybe, he would be caught up in his euphoria like the drug addicts I'd seen in the movies. Was I really ready to see him like this? Was I prepared to move from knowing (in my thoughts) he was a drug addict to actually seeing him as one? In a way I wanted to see him in such a light. Maybe it would help to justify the anger growing inside of me. But then again, I didn't want us to find him because he was my father. I wanted to—no I needed to—maintain some level of respect for him, didn't I? I guess it didn't matter one way or another, because we were in hot pursuit. I needed to be prepared for whatever state we found him whether I felt I was ready or not.

Each place we searched, daddy was nowhere to be found. All the people we encountered provided similar stories: "We haven't seen him; we don't know where he is . . ." I knew they were lying and so did mommy. At some point our search ended with no sign of my father.

My mind has blocked out how the evening ended. However, I am sure it wasn't pleasant. After all, we could not find daddy and mommy was angry and inebriated—a formula fit for disaster.

What Will Your Decision Be?

Inspired by my father, Mart Everson Jr.

I was fifteen when I first learned of my father's drug addiction. That summer, I wrote, *What Will Your Decision Be?* This poem was my endeavor to help my father understand what his addiction was doing to the family.

One hundred dollars for a ten-minute high,
Spending up your money, and you're just getting by.

Transform you it will; it's just that strong.
You're wasting your life on a high that's not long.

You're losing your wife and your kids are confused,
All because of the decisions you choose.

The young kids go blank; they can't understand.
You used to be daddy. Now you're just a strange man.

The older kids are shocked; they constantly try to cope.
They just can't believe that their father's on dope.

You've developed a problem that you always deny.
You really want to stop, but you haven't really tried.

The more you think about it, the more crack rocks you smoke.
Your wife's on the edge, and she's just about to croak.

She restrains the thought that her husband's an addict,
But after awhile she decides she won't have it.

She's tried too hard to make the marriage work.
All she gets back is the pain; and it hurts.

That addictive crack rock is truly on its way.
If you don't stop now, death will be the price you pay.

Was something so wrong that you had to turn to drugs?
Did you need more attention? Did you need more love?

Your family is in a daze. They want to know your problems.
The best thing is to tell them so they can help you solve them.

Just stop for a moment and look at yourself.
You have a serious problem and you won't go get help.

Think of the times your family's spent together.
If you improved your situation, your life would be much better.

It won't be easy because you have been using crack too long.
But all you have to do is be determined and be strong.

It may be dark now, but there's light up ahead.
There are bundles of joy for the tears that you've shed.

Just think of your future. You'll have a happy life.
Your kids saying, "Daddy" and a loving smile from your wife.

If you don't take the chance, do you think this will be?
Will there be other days that the Lord will let you see?

That's for you to decide; it's your destination.
It's up to you and your determination.

What Will Your Decision Be?
The Sequel

Inspired by my father, Mart Everson Jr.

I was seventeen when I scripted *What Will Your Decision Be? The Sequel*. My father agreed to enter a drug rehabilitation program, which he did not complete. My intent for this poem was to further explain the impact of his addiction on the family. Also, as his oldest child, I wanted to explain how I felt about the addiction.

You finally decided to confront your problems.
You've made an effort to try and solve them.

Rehab you say, so off you go.
But you realize this is not your type of show.

You're not accustomed to being so restricted.
The counselors are too stern, and you are not committed.

It won't hurt, you think, to make another effort.
So you try again to do and be better.

You prepare to escape your addictive condition.
Yet knowing that you would soon return to its destructive mission.

You do a great job playing your role,
All the while knowing the drug still has control.

You pretend to be a good man, a good husband, a good father.
But tell me this: why do you even bother?

You give into your habit. Again it takes control.
It destroys your good intentions and torments your soul.

Your family is outraged. They see the path you've paved.
They finally accept the fact that you have become a slave.

You tried to stop using. Your family gave you support and love.
You should have placed your case in the hands of God above.

You wanted to be your own lawyer and to present your case alone.
You wanted to be "da' man" and to do things on your own.

But as you know, nothing works properly without God in the plan.
All things belong to Him, and He holds the world in His hands.

Look at your kids. Are they proud to have a father like you?
Probably not based on the inconsiderate things you do.

Your second-oldest daughter has told you what she thinks.
But you brush her off and you continue to sink.

Your middle daughter dreams of a family that's complete.
But your actions beat you down and she sees your defeat.

Your one and only son is too young to cope.
Maybe it' because he's lost all hope.

Your baby girl doesn't know exactly what's going on.
But she is smart enough to know that daddy is always gone.

What will she think when she is old enough to see the big picture?
Will you see then that family and drugs aren't a fruitful mixture?

Oh! Your wife, your sweetheart, your good thing, your love.
She's been your moral supporter and beautiful black dove.

You have put her through the worst. You have done her wrong.
You have made her suffer greatly, but she still rises and strives on.

She has bent over backward to help you, love you, and be true.
But all you ever thought about was pleasing only you!

It's my turn, me, your oldest child.
I never said a word, but I think it's about time.

I was always quiet, holding my feelings inside,
Because I knew you would have just pushed them aside.

I'm fed up with your lifestyle. You need to get with the program.
The Lord's trumpet should move you not the devil's slow jams.

Almost three years later . . .

Where does it all end? Will you ever stop this ignorant way of life?
Or will you continue to live with the pain, struggle, and strife?

That's for you to decide; it's your destination.
It's up to you and your determination.

Chosen

Inspired by my father, Mart Everson Jr.

"For many are called, but few are chosen."
Matthew 22:14 (KJV)

At age twenty-five, I learned that my father did not complete another rehabilitation program. I recall writing *Chosen* while on a road trip. I was in the passenger seat wrestling in my mind and trying to calm my extremely heavy heart. I could not verbally articulate how I felt, so it was necessary for me to write. I wanted to let my father know that despite what he'd been through, he was not a lost cause. I wanted to inspire him to embrace God's will for his life. It is my earnest prayer that one day he will share his full testimony. I believe it will bring hope to the hopeless and eradicate bondage in the lives of those who are captive to drug addiction.

Years of running without direction yet praying for a director.
Months of hiding—yet wishing for a seeker.

Weeks of spending on crack while searching for an accountant.
Days of highs and lows, asking for someone to come in and stop it.

In darkness, you desired light. In despair, you desired to rejoice.
When your pit became too deep, you wanted a calming voice.

While in the grips of the adversary, you prayed to be a conqueror.
While under his influence, you visualized being an overcomer.

With a bound mind and heavy soul, you yearned for a release.
Your body was suffering, but you did not want to face defeat.

You dreamed of emerging into the man you used to be.
You wanted to make things right. You hoped others would see.

Everything you hoped for was there from the start.
Everything you needed was knocking at your heart.

Yes! It was God—your everything. He is your all and all.
It was He who sustained you. It is He who cushioned your falls.

God is the director. He will illuminate your path through life.
He is the seeker who will find you and lead you out of the night.

God is the accountant who will show you how to make a profit.
He will speak to your highs and lows. His spoken word will stop it.

Through Him you will gain the victory and be an overcomer.
For His word declares that you are more than a conqueror.

He will give you comfort and bring you peace.
He will ensure the work He began in you is full and complete.

God is calling forth the man He predestined you to be.
He will use your transformation to set others free.

He is purging and molding you by His fiery flame.
Reforming you for a testament of eternal change.

You are on a rigid course. Your mind is in the renewing stage.
You are being transformed. Your life is starting on a new page.

Today is the day. God has begun to make things right.
You have been called and chosen. Now mount up and take flight.

"... there is nothing covered, that shall not be revealed;
and hid, that shall not be known."
Matthew 10:26 (KJV)

The Secret Things

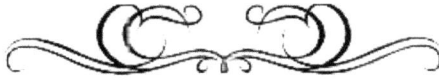

I use to wonder why she looked so disgusted when she saw him. It was as if he was a nasty disease she was determined not to catch. If she saw him walking on one side of the street, she'd cross over to the other side. If his name was mentioned, she had nothing to say—nothing good anyway. Everything she did concerning him was exaggerated and unwarranted in my eyes, because I didn't think he was that bad. Yeah, he smelled like alcohol, had bloodshot eyes more often than not, and was creepy in some ways. But overall, I thought he was okay until she revealed the secret things.

Broken Little Girl Destined to Be Whole

Inspired by my sister, Marquita Everson

She was a cute little girl, just as precious as could be.
She looked mixed. A black Indian maybe? Yeah, Cherokee.

Her black hair was slightly curly and her skin was somewhat light.
Her eyes were kind of dark, but ironically, they shone quite bright.

Ladylike, you could say. Strong personality and very outspoken.
Although she was vibrant, no one knew her spirit had been broken.

He lustfully looked upon her. An abomination his mind conceived.
He touched her in ways the normal mind would not believe.

"Don't tell anybody!" he'd say. "They'll kill me if you do.
Let's just keep what's going on here between me and you."

She was only a little girl, so she did what she was told.
She was tormented and cried inside. She didn't tell a soul.

Occurrence after occurrence. Filthy touch after filthy touch.
All she wanted to do was be a child. She didn't ask for much.

Despite the woman in his life, he still sought to violate innocence.
He had a serious problem. His actions defied what made sense.

Torment somewhat subsided as he stopped pursuing the little girl.
But the damage was done. The abuse adversely affected her world.

He went on with his life, but the little girl was not the same.
She was left to carry the burden of low self-esteem and shame.

Deep internal wounds gave way to toxic relationships with men.
To avoid possible loss, she always sought to please and keep them.

All the while she could hear her abuser, "Don't tell anybody."
His voice growing louder, "If you do, they'll kill me."

Men came and went; relationships went and came.
The past fueled her promiscuity as she camouflaged her pain.

The heavy burden forced her to reveal the cause of her torment.
She courageously faced her past and shed its shameful garment.

Despite her encounters, God had a divine plan for her soul.
That broken little girl was always destined to be whole.

"For I know the plans *and* thoughts that I have for you,' says the LORD, 'plans for peace *and* well-being and not for disaster to give you a future and a hope."
Jeremiah 29:11 (AMP)

". . . thou shalt be a good minister of Jesus Christ, nourished up in the words of faith and of good doctrine, whereunto thou hast attained."
I Timothy 4:6 (KJV)

Minister of the Gospel

She'd been teaching the Word of God for years and was now preparing to be elevated in the ministry. She was a little worried about the occasion. Of course, this was news to me, seeing that I'd witnessed her confidently stand before people, children and adults alike, to teach, preach, and sing. She went on to share that despite having plenty of experience in this area, it was somehow different this time. She was moving from sister to minister. Yes, she was the same person, but her responsibilities and function were about to shift. The weight of such a transition caused her to ask, "Who am I that you would choose me, Lord?" Her questions were fueled by feelings of unworthiness. Following our conversation, she went on to prepare for the ministerial licensing service, and I went on with the word "unworthy" resonating in my spirit. Not many days hence, an encouraging word flowed through my pen.

I was blessed to attend the licensing service. It was a monumental moment in her life. She preached her initial sermon (as did her husband--Uncle Jesse) and was presented as a minister of the gospel. The service was followed by a grand meal prepared by none other than Mother Doris "Doll" Jones. I call her Grandma Doll. As I watched the new minister interact with those in attendance, I sensed the dark cloud of unworthiness still looming.

When the last of Grandma Doll's chicken and collard greens were packed into the fridge and the dishes were washed and put away, I asked for a moment of the minister's time. In the basement of grandma's house, both her and Uncle Jesse stood by the table worn from the day's festivities. She laid her head on his shoulder—her eyes not far from closing. He pulled her close putting his tired arm around her waist, and they listened as I delivered the encouraging word.

Unworthy

Inspired by my aunt, Tammy Lyles

Unworthy, you say? Well, I must agree.
That's if you're talking about that nasty and undisciplined flesh.
But you've forgotten that the blood of Jesus saturates your life.
You are His righteousness.

Unworthy, you say? Then I say, yes.
That's if you're speaking of the carnal and worldly man.
But you've forgotten about the power of the Holy Spirit.
He infuses you and gives you strength to stand.

Unworthy, you say? You are absolutely right.
That's if you're speaking of the continually evil and wicked heart.
But you've forgotten about God's glory and its brilliance.
His everlasting light pierces through the deepest dark.

Unworthy, you say? Your diagnosis is accurate.
That's if you're talking about the intellectual mind.
But you've forgotten the miracle working words of Jesus.
They raised the dead, opened deaf ears, and gave sight to the blind.

Unworthy, you say? *No!* Unworthy you were.
It was part of your old nature and what you used to be.
But Jesus sacrificed His life and lovingly redeemed you.
It is because of Him that you are now worthy!

"He made Christ who knew no sin to [judicially] be sin on our behalf, so that in Him we would become the righteousness of God [that is, we would be made acceptable to Him and placed in a right relationship with Him by His gracious lovingkindness]."
2 Corinthians 5:21 (AMP)

**"Death is the grand entrance,
the door that swings into eternity."**
—Erwin W. Lutzer

In Loving Memory

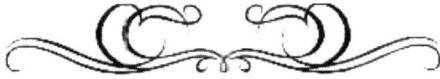

I was lying in the hotel bed immersed in sleep when my cell phone rang. Our summer vacation was over, and we were on our way back to our duty station in Hawaii. The family was aware of our schedule, so it was very strange for the phone to ring at this time of the morning. As my husband handed me the phone, I wondered who in the world it could be. Although I was half asleep, I was able to muster a comprehendible hello.

My mother's voice, hoarse from crying, came through the receiver and snatched me from that space between sleep and wakefulness. I was instantly alert and afraid to know why she was crying. "Andrea, your Aunt Dorothy passed away." I sat in the darkness listening to my mother's voice fade into the background as my thoughts grew louder and louder. *Aunt Dorothy, dead? This can't be! I was just with her the other day.*

The next morning, we boarded the plane as scheduled. We were heading to paradise (Hawaii), but I was in hell. The nagging ache in my heart caused me to contemplate what Aunt Dorothy's death really meant. As I pondered, I was moved to write.

I Have Learned

Inspired by my aunt, Dorothy Chandler

My heart aches as I write because you are no longer here.
My mind replays our last day together. My eyes well up with tears.

I remember the joy as we chatted of past memories.
The sound of your heartfelt laughter will always be dear to me.

As I hugged you at Grandma's, I didn't know it'd be the last time.
The thought of not seeing you again never once crossed my mind.

At the notice of your passing, I received a reality check.
I learned that life can turn out differently than we expect.

I expected you to be healed of lupus and share your testimony.
I expected you to grow old before being taken up to glory.

But God's perfect plan turned my expectations upside down.
I've learned a vital lesson since you've left to receive your crown.

I have learned that life is truly precious, and it is not a guarantee.
I have learned that God and His will should be our main priority.

So often we get caught up in the things of this present time.
What's most important gets lost and ultimately undermined.

We were called to be a light to a dying world that is dark and lost.
We were called to share the gospel no matter what the cost.

Your death has caused priorities to come into alignment for me.
It has reinstated God's most important purpose as my top priority.

You impacted me through your life and your death, as well.
You've inspired me to pursue higher heights and spiritually excel.

I thank God that through you I have truly been blessed.
May you bask in the glory of our Lord and enjoy your eternal rest.

"You shall rise before the gray-headed and honor the aged…"
Leviticus 19:32a (AMP)

Honor the Aged

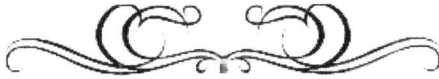

It is a tradition for my husband's family to celebrate Grandma Tot's birthday each year. In preparation for her 90th birthday, my mother-in-law, Peggy, asked me to write a tribute for the occasion. I was reluctant to accept and attempted to make every excuse possible not to do it. Momma Peggy would not take no for an answer. From the time she asked me to write the tribute up until one week before the birthday party, I was a mess. I wasn't convinced I could write something of value to compliment such a rich life and beautiful celebration. I had several other major projects vying for my attention and no matter how many times I attempted to write something, the words would not flow. I was also extremely nervous because not only did I have to write the tribute, I had to deliver it before a family audience—many of whom I'd never met before. My stomach was in knots. But Father God settled my soul long enough to think about Grandma Tot and her life. From that settled place, the tribute came forth.

No Less than Phenomenal

Inspired by Elouise C. Burney (Grandma Tot)

Short in physical stature but a giant in character; she is one of kind.
Envisioning this extraordinary woman brings many things to mind.

Mother to biological children. Nurturer to countless others.
Far-reaching influence qualifies her as a marvel and a wonder.

Watchful like an eagle and cool like the breeze.
Gentle as a dove and strong as oak trees.

Sweet like pie, keen, and wise.
Rich and extensive history can be seen in her eyes.

Her guidance yields growth. Her words produce life.
Her wisdom is expansive and it came with a price.

Experienced loss and suffered many defeats.
Scaled intimidating mountains with very high peaks.

Weathered nasty storms and faced innumerable fears.
Endured heartache in the valley and cried many tears.

Feet with many miles and a tongue with untold stories.
A face with a million smiles and an arsenal of testimonies.

Stability in chaos. Answers for the inquisitive.
Encouragement for those who are afraid to really live.

Pillar of hope that shouts, "Better days will come!"
A constant reminder that our work here isn't done.

She continues to hold tightly to God's unchanging hand.
With unwavering faith, she believes and stands.

She's worked hard, played hard, and loved hard, too.
She's been there, done that, and has the t-shirt, too.

Elouise C. Burney is amazing and truly remarkable.
She's incredible, astonishing, and no less than phenomenal.

"Because time itself is like a spiral, something special happens on your birthday each year: The same energy that God invested in you at birth is present once again."
—*Menachem Mendel Schneerson*

It's Your Birthday

The first time I visited Kingdom Outreach Ministries International (KOMI) during our tour in Okinawa, Japan, I was overtaken by how genuinely friendly everyone was. I didn't perceive any facades or ulterior motives—just people with a heart for God. The atmosphere was refreshing and conducive to receiving from the Lord.

There was one particular woman who stood out. She was a member of the praise and worship team. She seemed to literally be moved by the words of every song. It was as if she was having a service with the hosts of heaven all by herself. She had a loving and passionate aura about her. She sang with conviction and exhorted the congregation with God-confidence and fervency I hadn't seen in a while. As we transitioned from praise into worship, the melody played by the keyboardist instantly brought tears to her eyes. She had entered the holy of holies and was in the posture of worship before one word was ever uttered. It was clear she was a true worshipper. Unbeknownst to me, this woman was first lady of the house—the one who would eventually become my spiritual mother.

During the planning of Lady King's fiftieth birthday party, I was asked to write a poem for the occasion. Initially, I was hesitant to do so because I was unsure I could capture her essence only knowing her such a short time. However, after some persuading (thanks, Felicia) and reflection upon my observations and interactions with Lady King, it wasn't long before the words began to flow.

When You . . .

Inspired by my spiritual mother, Pastor Kimberly King

When you enter a room, your presence commands attention.
But it's not by pressure or force.
It's dynamite power penetrating from your yielded vessel.
God is your sovereign source.

When you speak, hearts are arrested and minds are captured.
You give Godly wisdom to those who'll listen.
Revelation knowledge fills the atmosphere.
You challenge the hearer to come higher, change, and transition.

When you move, it's with precision, not jagged motion.
No contradictory behaviors as to confuse the watcher.
Rather, it's Holy Spirit operating in and through you.
Showing forth the will and ways of the Master.

When you sing, the presence of God is ushered in.
Angels look to see who has taken their place at the throne.
Yokes are destroyed, and the bound become free.
They enter into a place of peace they've not previously known.

When you exhort, the spirit man rises from its defeated position.
It stands upright, shoulders back, and chest out.
When you fight, you strategically and fearlessly engage the enemy.
You demonstrate what spiritual warfare is really about.

When you cry, tears of compassion well up in your eyes.
They flow for the hurting, the broken, and the lost.
Your submission to God helps you bear the burden(s) of the weak.
Despite the heaviness, you remain faithful no matter the cost.

When you were born fifty years ago, God smiled real big!
He knew He'd fashioned an exceptional work of art.
You, God's masterpiece, would bring him glory and great joy.
For you came forth from his very own heart.

HAPPY 50TH BIRTHDAY LADY KING!

"In learning you will teach, and in teaching you will learn."
—*Phil Collins*

Teach Me

It was my first deployment or better yet my first work assignment abroad—two months in Kyrgyzstan. Ironically, I was no longer an active-duty Marine. I was now an Air Force civilian employee. I was convinced this assignment was going to be a much-needed change of pace since I'd be exempt from the normal requirements of family, work, and church. I was under the impression this was going to be a sabbatical of sorts. Boy, was I mistaken. Instead, I'd entered a season of teaching.

During my first week on the base, I met a young Airman who was on fire for the Lord. Her excitement concerning the things of God was similar to all who are fresh to the body of Christ. Do you remember how you wanted to run out and save the world when you first accepted Christ as Lord and Savior? You shared the message of salvation with any and everyone you came in contact with. Well, that was her. She would sing praises to the Lord all day long even though she wasn't anointed to sing (inside joke). She stayed on the mountaintop and felt all was well in the world, because she was saved. That was until the trials of life came.

She quickly started putting a demand on the well within me. Certainly, I was not looking for this to happen because I desired to be taught, not to teach. However, it became clear that God's plans had nothing to do with my plans. Gradually, I found myself lending a listening ear, imparting wisdom, and being used to assist in her growth and development as a child of God and as a young woman. When she approached me with questions, I'd give her scriptural and practical advice. But many times I was moved to simply say, *"Press."* The intent was to remind her that in the pressing, she was growing. In the pressing, God was developing her character.

It's funny how we have the tendency to think one-sided when it comes to those we are called to teach. Although we are helping them, the opportunity to do so is actually helping us. Needless to say, this Airman was not the only one to leave Kyrgyzstan a changed woman. I did too.

Press

Inspired by Jennifer "Jenny from the block" Noel

"I press toward the mark for the prize of the high calling
of God in Christ Jesus." *Philippians 3:14 (KJV)*

Keep your hand to the plow and don't you dare look back.
No matter what you are going through, be sure to stay on track.

The road ahead may look scary with its billowing and dark clouds.
Nonetheless, you need to press. Embrace what God allows.

Despite the hardships you face, set your mind to pass the test.
The prize of the high calling is yours if you trust God in the press.

"For they that have used the office of a deacon well purchase to themselves a good degree, and great boldness in the faith which is in Christ Jesus."
I Timothy 3:13 (KJV)

The Deacon

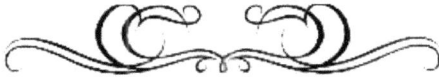

The instructor slowly rose from his seat with his materials and proceeded to the podium. His slow stride said he was in no hurry. But his eyes said he was determined and focused. His serious facial expression reminded me of an old school missionary Baptist church deacon. However, he had a modern-day twist evident by his creased jeans, starched shirt, and dress shoes. When he reached the podium, he neatly placed his materials on top and put his right hand into the pocket of his jeans. He scanned the congregation for a moment and in a cool, laid-back voice said, "How's everyone doin' this evenin'?" After a few general exchanges, he moved forward with the Bible study lesson from John Ortberg's book *If You Want to Walk on Water, You Have to Get out of the Boat.*

Walking on Water
Inspired by Deacon Russ Riggins (R^2)

If you want to walk on water, you gotta get out of the boat.
Forget about how it used to be.
Throw caution to the wind; keep your eyes on Jesus.
Envision the water beneath your feet.

Cry out to Jesus as Peter did,
"Lord, if it be you, then bid me come."
In faith, proceed. Don't rationalize.
Move toward the voice of the Son.

Disregard the raging waters and blowing winds.
Look past the rocking boat.
Set your sights on Jesus and Him alone.
Your faith in Him will keep you afloat.

Maintain your faith. Do not fear or doubt.
Your unrelenting trust in God be sure to keep!
For as soon as you give into what you see (water) and hear (wind),
You will begin to sink.

If you want to walk on water, you gotta get out of the boat.
Remember, comfort is not your friend.
The stretching of your faith is needful for growth.
It's the substance on which your advancement depends.

"And I will give you pastors according to mine heart, which shall feed you with knowledge and understanding."
Jeremiah 3:15 (KJV)

Good Shepherds

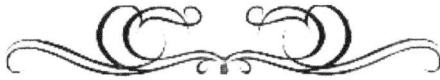

I wrote *"I Need You"* on February 23, 2005. In its original format, the dedication read, *"Inspired by those who have imparted into my life from the treasures of theirs!"* It was my attempt to show appreciation to all who participated in my growth and development—a declaration that I had not become the person I am without them. Although I hadn't previously shared the poem publically, May 2009 was the time for its release. During the pastoral appreciation ceremony, I specifically dedicated *"I Need You"* to my spiritual parents.

There are leaders in the body of Christ, who despite having a great anointing on their lives, stifle those under their care for fear of being outshined or outdone by them. Then there are leaders who see the greatness in others and without hesitation take on the responsibility of ensuring those individuals are developed into the men and women God has called them to be. Apostle Joseph King and Pastor Kimberly King have done this very thing in my life and the lives of countless others. I thank God for their sacrifice of love. Certainly, their hands-on involvement (along with several significant others) in my maturation process of life and ministry is a testament to the fact that we need one another.

I Need You

Inspired by all who imparted into my life from the treasures of theirs.
Dedicated to Apostle Joseph and Pastor Kimberly King

I need your experiences. I need your testimonies and your advice.
I need your friendship. I need your leadership and thoughts on life.

I need your love. I need your laughter. I need your courage.
I need your joy. I need your support when I'm discouraged.

I need your discipline. I need your rebuke and your correction.
I need your guidance. I need your wisdom and your direction.

I need your pain. I need your struggles. I need your tears.
I need your views and lessons learned throughout the years.

Use what's been firmly established inside of you to teach me.
Draw from the deep wells of your life so you can reach me.

Good, bad, and the ugly; the sum of you can make me wise.
You've been where I am going. Let me see life through your eyes.

The truth is, there's no making it through this life alone.
I need you, because I was never meant to do this on my own.

". . . If God be for us, who can be against us?"
Romans 8:31b (KJV)

Against All Odds

The call was heavy and great enough to cause a faith-filled child of God to possibly reconsider. After all, this young couple was as David in the eyes of a Goliath and as Nehemiah from the perspective of the saboteurs Sanballet and Tobiah. Most felt they were not old enough, strong enough, or wise enough to handle such an undertaking. However, against all odds, they stepped out and answered the call. Their faith and obedience serve as an example of what pleases the Lord and attracts His "Well done."

Well Done

Inspired by Pastor Jermaine and Lady Sa'Kina Ballenger

You accepted the assignment with reservations.
But you took it nonetheless.
Timid and uncertain in one-way or another,
Wondering how you'd pass the test.

You obediently launched out into the deep.
At God's Word, you dropped your nets.
Although you couldn't see the end results,
You still entrusted God with your "Yes".

There were times you considered giving up,
Crying out for the season of stretching to leave.
But the grace of God kept you pressing toward the mark.
To Him you continued to cleave.

Amid the faith-building trials and loud voices of the naysayers,
You steadfastly held your ground.
Despite the demands and weight of ministry,
From your wall you refused to come down.

You rolled up your sleeves and dug in for the night,
Pitching a tent at the place of God's choosing.
Determined to see God's will manifest;
You counted it an honor to do His bidding.

The curtains have closed on this season of growth,
Which has most certainly been a trying and needful one.
Yet you remained faithful and committed to the call.
For that, the Father says, "Well done!"

"Well done, my son, well done, my daughter.
Know that your labor was not in vain.
Much will be birthed out of your obedience.
Now I release you to experience the natural and spiritual gain."

"Those who bring sunshine to the lives of others cannot keep it from themselves."
—James Matthew Barrie

You Inspire Me

Throughout the years, many have provided general encouragement as it pertains to pursuing what God has given me to do. However, there are those who went beyond general encouragement. They pushed me into destiny even when they were not aware of it. Some verbally stayed on my case about publishing what God had given me. Others shared key information about writing, publishing, and God's intended purpose for my writing. And then there were those who motivated me by example through relentless pursuit of their God-given assignments. They planted seeds of possibility within me when I did not have the faith to believe beyond my self-imposed borders. Those seeds have been watered, and God is bringing forth the increase. I extend a special thanks to you for inspiring me!

Thank You

Aunt Tammy Lyles
Aunt Zera Southward
Marquita Everson
Kristina Everson
Arloishia Israel
Peggy Purdy
Tina Bloodsaw
Adele Simmons
Torie & Kisha Williams
Mia Gray
Khara Campbell
Uncle Major & Aunt Vanessa Warren
Lamont & Linda Warren
Apostle Joseph & Pastor Kimberly King
Pastor Vincent & Lady Valicia Smith
Damien Lee & Tannis Villanova
Veneta White
Nicole Boone
Luther & Deon Catchings
Pastor Darnella Walker-Allen
Bishop Michael & Evangelist Catherene Wyckoff
Renee Joseph
Danielle Land
Felicia Smith
Sondretta Graham
Tanya Gilliam
Danielle Knowles
Apostle Theresa Harvard-Johnson &
The Voices of Christ Leaders & Army
LaShaun O'Bryant
Darius "BooDaddy" Carr
Daryl & Leia Towe
Benford Stellmacher Jr.

About the Author

Andrea is a proven servant-leader with over twenty years of ministry and marketplace experience.

She has faithfully served the body of Christ in various capacities to include choir, youth and young adult ministries, hospitality, usher board, administration, finance, intercessory prayer, and leadership.

As a professional, Andrea was an active duty Marine and a government auditor with the Air Force Audit Agency. She is the founder of Kingdom Ventures LLC, a single source business and management consulting company where she acquaints people, businesses, and organizations with their potential. She is also the founder of Life Keys Training Center, an organization she established to help unlock and develop whole people who impact and transform their respective areas of influence for the Kingdom of God.

Andrea holds a Bachelors of Science in Accounting from Hawaii Pacific University, a Masters of Business Administration from Webster University, and a certification to teach *The Scribal Anointing*® from The Voices of Christ Apostolic-Prophetic School of the Scribe (APSOTS). She will become a certified coach with the John Maxwell Team in August 2018.

Andrea is a Syracuse, New York native. She has two children and resides in Waldorf, MD with her husband Telly.

Other books by Andrea

Come Forth: From the Shadows into View
A Poetry Collection

To order additional copies of this book and other books written by Andrea or for more information about Andrea's initiatives, visit:

www.thepropheticpen.com
www.lifekeystrainingcenter.com
www.kingdomventuresllc.com

Disclaimer: Each individual mentioned and/or reflected in a photograph gave the author permission to include his or her name and image in this book. For the deceased, the author used personal memories and photograph.

For more information about *The Scribal Anointing*® and its progenitor, Apostle Theresa Harvard Johnson, visit:

The Voices of Christ Apostolic-Prophetic School of the Scribe
www.thescribalanointing.com

The Chamber of the Scribe
www.chamberofthescribe.com

The Scribal Realm of Dreams and Visions
www.thescribalrealm.com

The Scribal Arsenal
www.bookstore.schoolofthescribe.com

www.ingramcontent.com/pod-product-compliance
Lightning Source LLC
Chambersburg PA
CBHW060412050426
42449CB00009B/1956